Straight From the Heart

Roger D. Johnston

Cadmus Publishing
www.cadmuspublishing.com

✦ III ✦

DEDICATION

This book is for all the people who have made me a better person. First of all, my Lord Jesus Christ for putting the words in my heart to write this book. My son Toby whom I love with all my heart, my big brother Timothy and my good friends Genni and Louise for all their help and support in getting this book done.

Roger

ACKNOWLEDGEMENT

Many people have helped in developing this book by their prayers and encouragement to keep writing and to continue to listen to God for the words to make this book come to reality.

I want to send a special thanks to Genni and Lousie for all their help for without these two ladies this book would not have been possible. So, thank you both very much, you both are loved.

I also want to send a special thanks to my big brother Timothy who has given me so much encouragement to keep on writing even though I wanted to stop, so Timothy thank you for all the encouraging words I love you very much big brother.

Roger

INTRODUCTION —

Your spiritual life no matter your religion or race is not a hobby or a job from which you can take a vacation, it's the source of your life. Yes, there is a purpose for your life, and I hope and pray that you have or will learn that purpose so that you can go out and help others learn their purpose.

As you know there is no neutral ground, either you are moving forward or you are a moving backwards, yes, there is a temptation to coast, to rest on your spiritual tree, but if you wouldn't choose to do that for three, six, or twelve months why would you choose to do it for a day? So don't be a know it all even for a day because you cannot depend on yesterday's faith to meet tomorrow's challenges.

Physically life can be a challenge I know from experience when I lost my family and freedom due to being incarcerated and believe me that was a huge challenge and I wanted to just give up, but I'm here today to encourage you to consider wherever you are in your spiritual life bring intelligence, talent, giftedness, wisdom and how-to-experience to those you come in contact with.

No matter where you are in your life you must never give up your sense of purpose. The more you live the more you have to offer, so let me suggest four ways to offer what you know. #1) Be open to learn; #2) Be open to new experiences; #3) You also need to be open to teach and #4 (which I believe is the most important of them all) BE OPEN TO LOVE.

Life is a journey and sometimes the journey is joyful, inspiring, and fulfilling. At other times it's a difficult struggle. We've all experienced winding roads and frustrating detours along the way. Everyone knows about stumbling blocks, disappointments, and losses. We all face problems and pressures, fears and frustrations, struggles and setbacks, and I believe it's important to be aware of what's happening in our lives and to reflect on our experiences so that we can learn and grow as a result.

At some point I think just about everybody has been tempted to give up, throw in the towel, I know I have, but I'm here to tell you "DON'T DO IT" treasure your dreams and work so they come true. Life can be very difficult at times, stress can mount up to where sometimes it's hard to see the light at the end of the tunnel, but the light is there.

You may be in a difficult place right now, but new doors will be opened for you to walk through and remember you're not alone, you have family, friends and other people to walk with you through those doors, you do not have to go about it alone so don't let your dreams die because of fear of being alone.

Whatever your belief may be, stir up your faith, fan the flame of the spirit who lives in you! Remember I said don't depend on yesterday's faith to meet tomorrow's challenges, and always remember what brought you to where you are, will not take you to where you need to be. So be thankful for your memories but don't settle down there. Be grateful for what you've already learned but you can't be satisfied with it, you need to constantly learn more. You've already learned a lot now it's time to put it all into action and remember you will never change your life until you change something you do daily.

You would not be human if you sometimes didn't wish that you could just start over again, we've all made some rotten decisions, we've said and done things for which we're now ashamed, and if given the opportunity we would just blot those thing's off the record. Well now is the time for you to start over. Wherever you may go continue to help others grow in their faith or beliefs and help them to start over as well.

Writing the words in this book has been a wonderful journey and I wish you all well on your continued journey to freedom, forgiveness, and hope as you read this book. Wherever you find yourself on your spiritual journey find the courage to take the next step. A long journey begins with a single step and I want to congratulate you all for taking that first step, and remember just like the seals say, the only easy day was yesterday, so before I go always remember you have 100% successfully overcame your failures because you are still standing today.

Good Luck & Thank You
Roger

Table of Contents

THINKING OF YOU

Here I am on this cold winter night,
Laying here wondering if you're alright.

I miss your body next to mine,
Keep telling myself things will be fine.

I pray to God asking to show me a way,
To help me write the things I need to say.

I miss you so much I wish you knew,
Just hang in there God will help you through.

I promise you now that I won't be long,
So, keep your head up and stay strong.

I just want you to know that I love you so,
Just wanted to tell you that before I go.

So, goodnight to you and sweet dreams too,
Always remember I'm thinking of you . . .

PHONE CALL

Hello God, I called to talk to you for a while,
For I have a frown to turn into a smile.

You see I can't seem to make it on my own,
I need your love, so I'll never be alone.

Give me faith dear God to get through the day,
And not to worry about things in any way.

I ask you dear God to keep my family safe and sound,
give them confidence for whatever fate they're bound.

Thank you, God, for taking this call,
and for your love when I stumble and fall.

Your number is the one that answers every time,
never get a busy signal, never paid a dime.

Thank you for listening to my pain and sorrow,
goodnight God, I love you, I'll call again tomorrow . . .

LOVE NOTE

I start this note with hello, how do you do,
just a few lines to let you know I love you.

I want you to know I miss you so much,
wish I was there to feel your touch.

I know one thing and one thing only,
I'm here all alone and feel so lonely.

Thank you for being there during the hard times,
I thank God every day for letting you be mine.

So don't you worry dear it won't be too long,
just hold your head up and always stay strong.

I thought I would write this for you today,
and tell you I love you on the way.

The love I have "oh" it's so so true,
believe me dear it's all just for you . . .

THE PROMISE

Come to me now and let me get started,
for I see that you are broken hearted.

I am the one who can guide you through,
and I am here just for you.

All you have to do is trust in me,
and I will show you what your life can be.

So, what do you think will you give it a try,
if you don't, I'm afraid you will cry.

It's not hard to ask me for my help,
for I want you to know the promise I have kept.

I promise you now I will always be there,
and I promise to you I will be fair.

So come on over and let me help you,
for there's so much to do before I'm through . . .

THE SWORD

When things in life seem to get rough,
just remember one thing, you're not so tough.

You can always take it straight to the Lord,
And He will fight for you with His sword.

If you're not sure at what you should do,
just ask the Lord and he will show you.

So when you're lost and feel all alone,
just pray to God to take you home.

You should know that He can do all things,
so open your eyes to see the love God brings.

So take His sword and fight the good fight,
and always remember God will show what's right.

So when you need help go to God in prayer,
and open your heart and accept His share . . .

THICK AND THIN

Hello my love how are you today,
wish I was there for I have so much to say.

I will love you forever through thick and thin,
and baby I'm not just saying it with this pen.

You mean so much to me, you fill my heart,
as strong as my love is we will never part.

What do you think, can we get through it all,
even if one of us stumbles and take a fall.

I will be there to catch you if ever you do,
and to hold you and show you how I love you.

I just wanted you to know what you mean to me,
as long as we have love then things could be.

So, goodbye for now my dear sweetheart,
just wanted to say my love will never fall apart . . .

THE PRICE

I will trust in you Lord with all my heart,
for you are the one who gave me this start.

You said I could call upon you when I have a need,
will you Lord, once again plant your seed.

You have helped me through thick and thin,
even helped me while I'm here in the pen.

I need your help Lord just once again,
show me now how this life should begin.

You took my problems and now I have none,
and all this was done through your only begotten SON.

I thank you Lord for your Son Jesus Christ,
for I know He didn't have to pay that price.

I know the price was high for Him to pay,
and I know you hear me whenever I pray . . .

OUR LOVE

My life is not complete without you by my side,
the love I have for you I cannot hide.

You mean more to me than you really know,
so open your heart baby and let the love flow.

I think about you each and every day that goes by,
not being there with you "well" I just want to cry.

So I hope you understand when I say I love you,
and always believe me when it's said it's true.

I'm asking you now baby just hang in there,
our hearts are broken because we really do care.

My hands are wide open so put yours in mine,
together we will be all in due time.

Our love grows stronger each and every day,
and I will always be with you leading the way . . .

THE PRAYER

I start this prayer with Lord please help me,
for I am a baby and need your help to see.

I don't know what daddy has done wrong,
but I'm asking you Lord please don't take long.

Bring my daddy home to me to stay,
For I am sure he will change his way.

Tell him for me that I love him too,
and show him Lord that your love is true.

Will you let him know that I miss him so,
"oh" there's one more thing Lord before I go.

Protect him and guide him down the right road,
and let him know that you carry the load.

Thank you, dear God, for taking this prayer,
for I know for sure that you are there . . .

THIS ONE TIME

I'm writing to you to let you know,
that I love you very much and miss you so.

I am so sorry for I know what I did was wrong,
can't help thinking of you when I hear our song.

So will you forgive me just this one time,
and I promise you dear thing's will be fine.

My heart is broken I can't stand it anymore,
I have cried so much that my head is sore.

I want you to know I didn't mean to hurt you,
because this love I have for you is so true.

So I'm asking you dear just this one time,
asking you to let me know you're doing fine.

Thank you, my love, for you are so kind,
and I promise you now this is the last time . . .

IT'S FREE

I want you to know His salvation is free,
so reach out your hand because it's for thee.

So look up to the Lord and take His Hand,
and by doing that then you know you can.

You can be free from deep inside,
for God is with you then you know you can.

You can be free from deep inside,
for God is with you He can't hide.

He gives you salvation because He loves you,
and all He wants from you is to be true.

So grab hold of God's sweet love,
let Him make you white as a dove.

He will take your troubles till you have none,
for His salvation has made you, His son.

It's all free just for you and me,
just open your heart and let it be . . .

TAKE A LOOK

Forgive me lord God for I am a sinner,
take my hand now because I'm a beginner.

I promise you now I will do my best,
I will work for you Lord and never rest.

Can you Lord take away all this pain,
for I need you with me before I go insane.

So I'm asking you Lord to take a new look,
to make sure my name is in your book.

I am sure that you have written it in there,
for you have promised that you would be fair.

I now know it's true that I can always be,
just as long as you are always with me.

So thank you Lord for what you have done,
for taking my hand and making me your son . . .

GOD'S HAND

What can I say to help you understand,
your life and troubles are in God's hand.

I told you before, He died on that cross,
for you and I because we were lost.

He is the only one who can get us through,
for the love He has it's for me and you.

Just go to God and ask Him please,
come down to help you meet your needs.

He is my provider and my protector too,
and I am sure He would be the same for you.

So open your heart and let the Lord in,
for He promised you forgiveness for your sin.

I thank you now for giving your time,
now God's love and grace will make you shine . . .

MY ANGEL

You are my angel I want you to know,
and always remember that I love you so.

I miss your hugs and your goodnights too,
one day soon I will be with you.

You are my angel I just wanted you to know,
there's one more thing before I go.

Daddy will love you always to the very end,
and I promise I'm not just saying it with this pen.

So goodnight to you and sweet dreams too,
don't forget daddy's thinking of you.

My little angel you mean the world to me,
"that" I hope you will always see . . .

TEARS

You are my baby I love you so,
but I don't think I can let you go.

Please my darling come back to me,
and I promise you that things could be.

Hello baby, what do you say,
can I come home to you to stay.

We've seen the days we've seen the years,
I miss you so much it brings me to tears.

I'm so sorry for hurting you,
I just want you to know my love is true.

I keep thinking about our very first date,
and I do believe you were running late.

I love you baby, I love you so,
but I don't think I can let you go . . .

BRIGHTEST STAR

Whenever I look up to the sky,
the brightest star makes me want to cry.

It makes me think of my Lord Jesus Christ,
God's only begotten Son who paid a great price.

When I look up and see that star,
I know for sure that God's not far.

He didn't have to die that day on that cross,
but He did it for me because I was lost.

So I thank you Father for sending Him to me,
to open my eyes so I could see.

Now that I have Him, I'll never let go,
for there's so much more I need to know.

I will fight each battle with His sword,
for I now belong to Jesus Christ my Lord . . .

BROTHER

You are a brother that anyone would want,
wish I would have listened when you said don't.

I wouldn't trade you, not even a bit,
when we became brothers, I knew that was it.

So I want to thank you now at this time,
don't you worry bro, things will be fine.

You are the best I wish you knew,
and you're my brother and I love you.

I don't know what else I can say,
but whatever you do stay that way.

I want you to know you mean a lot to me,
so will you open your eyes so you can see.

I thank you now for helping me through,
don't ever forget "Brother" I love you . . .

IN GOD WE TRUST

In God we trust all through the years,
for you see, he takes away all our fears.

You have taken Him out of the schools today,
even took the right for our kids to pray.

They go to ball games without a prayer,
can't even ask God if He could be there.

What you're doing, you know it's not right,
so our prayer today is, God show your light.

We need God in each and every school,
for without Him there, these kids act a fool.

So what do you say, can we give them the right,
to pray to God for His Guiding Light.

We've always said In God We Trust,
so prayer in schools "well" it's a must.

Bring it back to our kid's today,
let them all have the right to pray . . .

LITTLE NOTE

You are my son I love you so,
That I sure hope you already know.

I think about you every day that goes by,
Son, I miss you I just want to cry.

Daddy will love you to the very end,
I promise you that son not only with pen.

You are my only little bright star,
Just remember this son daddy's not far.

So whenever you need me I will be there,
For I love you so much, I really do care.

I just want you to know I miss you so,
And I want to say I love you before I go.

So I end this little note with a goodnight,
Sure I wish I was there son to hold you tight . . .

MY VALENTINE

I come to you today asking for your heart,
I want you to be mine and always be a part.

I'm asking you dear to be my Valentine,
will you give me your heart, I'll give you mine.

So I give to you this little Valentine note,
for I have so many hugs and kisses to tote.

Will you be mine on this special day,
put your hand in mine and I'll take you away.

I send with this note a hug and kiss too,
for I want my Valentine to be only you.

Down comes the angel of love to guide you,
to help make this Valentine dream come true.

So I'm asking you again to be my Valentine,
for I want nothing more but for you to be mine . . .

MY GRANDMA

You are the sweetest grandma on the face of the earth,
you were always there for me from the day of birth.

I don't know what I would do if I didn't have you,
for you took my hand and guided me through.

You are the best that anyone can get,
and I love you grandma just for it.

You were always there for my pain and sorrows,
never turned me away until tomorrow.

I wouldn't trade you for anything at all,
for I know you will be there if ever I fall.

So I thank you grandma for being so kind and sweet,
having you as my grandma I think is neat.

I just wanted to send this little note to you,
to tell you grandma just how much I love you . . .

IT'S NO GAME

Whenever you feel all down and lonely,
remember there's one way and one way only.

We always know when we done something bad,
for we can't get through it without being sad.

I'm asking you to join me so we can be the same,
I tell you now that this is no game.

We all need to be like Jesus Christ,
for let me tell you, He paid a great price.

So come with me to take God's hand,
and He will give to us His Promise Land.

I don't know about you, but I want Him in sight,
then I know for sure I will be safe at night.

Come on now and see what God has done,
so that we can be just like Jesus His Son . . .

JUST TRY

I want you to know it's not cool drinking,
for when you do, you're not thinking.

When you drink and drive you can take a life,
for all you know it could be your wife.

You know what you're doing that it is wrong,
and if you don't stop then it won't be long.

One of these days you're going to get caught,
and then you will swear it wasn't your fault.

So what do you say will you give it a try,
because what you're going it makes people cry.

I'm asking you now to please put it down,
stop drinking and driving and acting like a clown.

Just try one time not to go wild,
for the life you save could be a child . . .

BROKEN HEART

I come to you Lord with a broken heart,
asking you now for a brand-new start.

Be my leader each and every day,
open my eyes to show me the way.

Lift me up and put me on cloud nine,
for I opened my heart and said you're mine.

Now take my hand Lord and please guide me,
for my heart is broken can't you see.

I need you more than anything on earth,
because I was lost from the day of birth.

So here I am now all torn apart.
praying to you Lord to heal my heart.

I get out of bed and down on my knees,
asking you Lord to help me please.

The Lord said, I'm with you now from this day on,
for a sincere heart you have shown . . .

CALL ON ME

When you're out in the world to run about free,
remember my child it's easy to forget me.

You pray to me asking to make you right,
and I'm standing right here in your sight.

Just have faith and believe with all your heart,
that I am here doing my part.

You're not out there all alone,
each step you take, you're closer to home.

Why don't you now just call on me,
and open your heart to let it be.

All I want is for you to become mine,
and I promise you child everything will be fine.

So call on me and become my child,
put the world behind you and stop running wild.

You came this far asking to be free,
and I thank you child for calling on me . . .

CROSS MY HEART

I cross my heart and promise too,
to always worship and serve only you.

I am nothing without you by my side,
and I know now why Jesus died.

He came down to grab hold of me,
for I was blind and could not see.

I love you Lord I cross my heart,
and I thank you now for doing your part.

I know now what it is you mean,
for the price He paid I have seen.

Now that I see how I would turn out,
It's time to see what Jesus is all about.

I just hope I can spread the good news,
for a person like me I'm sure God can use.

So here I am Lord wanting to do my part,
and I will never forsake you I cross my heart . . .

DADDY'S CHAIR

Dear God, how long is it going to be,
before you bring my daddy home to me.

I miss him a lot this you should know,
there's one more thing God before I go.

Just let daddy know he's in my prayer,
and while he's gone, I sit in his chair.

I am sad each day that he is gone,
please God let him know he is not alone.

Tell him for me that I love him very much,
and that I miss him and his Father's touch.

Show him now that I really do care,
and before I go to bed I pray by his chair.

Thank you, God, for lending your ear,
just let my daddy know my love is dear . . .

GIVE IT UP

Here it is another day gone by,
I'm asking my Lord one question "WHY",

He tells me son just wait your turn,
unless you want to go to hell and burn.

I will wait Lord as long as it takes,
for I know for sure it's the best decision to make.

You told me before time and time again,
give it all to you and my new life will begin.

So here I am Lord giving it all to you,
asking you now to make me new.

I have faith and believe with all my heart,
that the promise you made, you will do your part.

I thank you Lord from deep inside,
for one day soon I will be at your side . . .

GOODNIGHT

Dear Lord God, I pray to thee,
grab my heart and please help me.

I feel much better than I did yesterday,
maybe God heard me when I prayed.

I pray really hard Lord as you know,
but one more thing Father before I go.

I ask you for your love and your wisdom,
for one day I want to live in your kingdom.

Then I opened my eyes to a great surprise,
there stood God's angel staring me in the eyes.

I was told no matter how hard I prayed,
God sent His Son, and the price was paid.

I got through the day with God on my heart,
thinking you Lord for doing your part.

So I pray to you to make me right,
ending this prayer with I love you and goodnight . . .

LITTLE PRAYER

Here it is the middle of an October day,
trying to think of something to say.

Closing my eyes to say a little prayer,
asking my Father to please be fair.

Dear Lord God, are the words that came out,
when that was said I began to shout.

Then I heard, get ready for my Salvation,
for you will go through each section.

Now here comes my wisdom, knowledge, and understanding,
so brace yourself and get ready for the landing.

Now I'm asking to show me the right road,
and you said to me son, you have been told.

Stay in my word and remember this little prayer,
and I promise you my child I will be there.

So this is my little prayer to you today,
asking you Lord to show me your way . . .

LOST SINNER

Dear Lord God, I start this prayer,
please hear me and help me be fair.

As you know I have so many needs,
I'm praying to you Lord asking on my knees.

You know what I need before I even start,
for you know everything that's in my heart.

You see God I have nowhere else to turn,
If I don't come to you, I'll go to hell and burn.

I'm lost as anyone else can ever be,
so I'm asking you God to please save me.

Thank you, dear God, for what you have done,
for letting this sinner become your son . . .

NO DOUBT

When things in life seem to occur,
there's one thing we can know for sure.

God our Father, He will help us out,
that my friend there is no doubt.

All you need to do is ask Him please,
and have faith that He will meet all your needs.

So just remember each and every night,
to ask God our Father to shine His light.

You may ask if the Lord will be fair,
I promise you; He will always be there.

So what do you say will you give it a try,
open your heart and quit being shy.

He doesn't care what the situation is,
he just wants you to become His.

So will you join me in this little prayer,
to ask God our Father to please do His share . . .

OPEN DOOR

Here I am now knocking on your door,
just as I have time and time before.

I am Jesus, God's only begotten Son,
open your eyes to see what I've done.

I died on a cross and shed my blood for you,
to cleanse your heart and make it new.

So here I am now in your broken heart,
and will always be here doing my part.

There will be times you just can't make it,
just remember I'm helping, and I don't mind a bit.

I'm so happy that you came to me,
that you opened your heart to let it be.

Thank you, child, for opening your door,
I promise to love you forever and more . . .

TAKE MY HAND

When the Lord speaks to you,
believe what I say for it is true.

I say these things to put in your heart,
to let you know that I'm doing my part.

What I tell you it's for your own good,
for I'm here helping you to live the way you should.

Don't you dare hide under that tree,
for I am here to set you free.

You've been a sinner from the very start,
now it's time for me to clean that heart.

So you see what it is I need to do,
I need to show you how I love you.

So take my hand and let me guide you,
and our life together will always be true . . .

TEACH ME

Dear God teach me today how shall I pray,
for I miss my daddy and I need him home today.

You see he has done something very wrong,
and I'm asking you Lord don't make it long.

I love him you know with all my heart,
so I'm praying to you Lord to do your part.

I don't know what I should ask of you,
but I know for sure that you will come through.

So teach me Lord what I should pray,
for I need my daddy home with me to stay.

Now here I am down on my little knees,
crying to you God and asking you please.

Here's my prayer to you today,
bring my daddy home to me to stay . . .

THE CRY

I want to say something important to you,
and believe me friend what I say is true.

There is another way I'm sure you know,
drinking and driving is not the way to go.

So why don't you think just for a while,
cause when you do, it can make someone smile.

I want you to know that it is wrong,
and if you keep doing it, it won't be long.

You should know that it can take a life,
if you're not careful it could be your wife.

So will you please give it a try,
for what you're doing it makes people cry.

There is help that you can get,
just ask me friend I don't mind a bit.

So don't drive while you're out there drinking,
for if you do, you're not really thinking . . .

TRUE LOVE

I want you to know that I love you,
and to let you know the love is true.

Just close your eyes and let me show thee,
what our life together will always be.

You mean so much I want you to know,
now that I have you, I'll never let go.

You are my one and only true love,
you shine just like God's pretty dove.

Even though we are far far apart,
you are always with me in my heart.

I want to make you happy as anyone can be,
for the love will last for you and me.

So open your heart so that you can know,
for I have so much love I need to show . . .

WHENEVER I FALL

It's hard to get through each and every day,
if you don't know God and His way.

You see it's hard to do things by myself,
for when I do there's nothing but problems left.

So I need your love to get through this mess,
for each question I ask, your answer is yes.

Protect me God and guide me through it all,
be there for me whenever I fall.

I'm not strong yet as I should be,
so I'm asking you Father to stay with me.

Give to me everything that I will need,
put in me now your one and only seed.

Thank you, Father, for your love and help,
you took my problems and them you have kept . . .

YOUR TURN

Here I am again all alone,
asking the Lord to take me home.

I have been told it's not your turn,
before you leave there's a lesson to learn.

I don't know what it is I can do,
but if God is in it then it's true

I was trying to do it all by myself,
then someone told me Jesus hasn't left.

So I lay at your feet today,
giving it all up to have your way.

I don't know what I can do,
so here I am Lord trusting in you.

Then the Lord said it's not my turn,
for you still have a valuable lesson to learn . . .

ALWAYS BELIEVE

Every now and then I begin to cry,
then I pray to the Lord asking why.

I was told when I pray to always believe,
for God is with me and will never leave.

So here I am giving you my heart,
knowing for sure I will get a new start.

I have faith as strong as can be,
"oh" dear Lord God please forgive me.

He said child your sins are now forgiven,
for Jesus died to make you and me even.

Just remember when you pray to me,
to ask what you like and always believe.

So I'm asking you Lord from deep inside,
to come be with me and stand by my side.

So you see what it is you need to do,
always believe that God will come through . . .

FOREVER FRIENDS

I'm writing to you this little note today,
for I have something I need to say.

You are a friend that anyone would want,
wish I knew what to say but I don't.

So I will just let you know this one little thing,
look at what a good friendship can bring.

I want to tell you what our friendship means to me,
so sit right down and get ready to see.

A friend will be there in a time of need,
never leave you hanging and never leave.

They will be there through thick and thin,
believe me friend I'm not just saying it with pen.

So your friendship means the world to me,
I just hope that it will last and always be . . .

LAST GOODBYE

Hey, Hey listen to me for I have something to say,
just in case you didn't know there's another way.

I hope you know that they will kill you,
you don't need drugs to get you through.

If you keep on doing them and keep getting high,
your family could be saying their last goodbye.

So I'm asking you now to take a look back,
to see what it is that you lack.

I don't know what else I can do,
but I can say there is help for you.

So I'm asking you now to look deep inside,
for what you're doing a lot of people died.

What do you think will you stop being a clown,
make yourself happy by putting them down . . .

ALL I EVER WANTED

All I ever wanted was a son to call my own,
then you finally came and turned this house into a home.

Because you were my son I planned for your great success,
nothing could be to good when you deserved only the best.

You became a handful, but I was always there,
problem after problem yet this one we cannot share.

I swore to do for you all those things never done for me,
I wanted you to be everything that you had dreamed.

So I give to you this day all the love I can give,
for I am always with you in your wonderful life to live.

I wish that I could do more each and every day,
all I can do for you son is guide you through the way.

All I ever wanted was a son to call my own,
I'm so happy that you came to turn this house into a home . . .

YOU'RE THE BEST

I ask myself this question and I'll let you know,
what my sister means to me before I go.

She is a person who will listen every time,
then she tells me that things will be just fine.

I don't know what I would do without her by my side,
guess I could find me a rock and try to hide.

She has all the love that I can give today,
I sure wish I knew just what to say.

I just want you to know sis, that you mean a lot to me,
and I promise that is how it always will be.

Hold on there, sister, before you go rest,
I want you to know that you're the best.

You see what it is that my sister means to me,
and I know that's the way it will always be . . .

KNOCKING

I will love you Lord forever and more,
yes, I hear you knocking on my door.

I will let you in so that I may see,
the wonderful life you have for me.

I will live this life just for you,
for you will always be there to help me through.

I will be a soldier and always fight,
to keep you Lord always in my sight.

You say you hear me when I pray,
I thank you Lord for I have a lot to say.

I ask you now to always guide me,
for my heart will always love thee.

I know you hear Lord what I ask of you,
so will you be with me and help me through . . .

NEVER LATE

Confusion my friend is not the way to go,
for all that does is sit you on low.

You need to remove all the old from the mind,
and always remember that God is so kind.

He is working with you to get you straight,
he knows what he's doing He is never late.

So turn right around and look Satan in the face,
and let him know that God is in this race.

You will always be the first to cross that line,
for God will be with you each and every time.

So whatever you do just get rid of the confusion,
because I know that you are tired of losing.

Now I want you to take God's sweet blessing,
just remember this is your number one lesson . . .

WALK WITH US

You know what it is that we lack,
that's asking Jesus to cover our back.

So will you Jesus come walk with us,
we promise you, we want to put up a fuss.

Do we really know what we need these days,
I think we need to know what Jesus will say.

If we listen and open our ear,
we will find out that Jesus is near.

We should know that He paid for our sin,
just for us all to be His next of kin.

If we ask Him to come down and give us help,
he will be with us for that promise he has kept.

So we need to ask Him just one time,
to change our life and make thing's fine.

We thank you Jesus for what you done for us,
and we are sorry for putting up such a fuss . . .

IT'S COMPLETE

You are my life and make me complete,
with you as my sweetheart "oh" it's so neat.

I will love you dear till death do us part,
even then you will always be in my heart.

So what I'm saying at this very time,
with you in my life I know thing's will be fine.

I will be there for you if ever you fall,
will be next to you just like waiting for a call.

I'm telling you right now that I love you dear,
losing you in life is what I fear.

So what I'm saying is I'll always be with you,
loving you sweetheart all the way through.

You are my life and I now know it's complete,
for you are my sweetheart and it's so neat . . .

HEAVEN'S BEST

One starry night the heavenly angels came out,
all they could do was yell and shout.

They fell to their faces they were paralyzed with fear,
the heavenly messenger reassured them as he drew near.

There was no royal procession no diamond signet ring,
no media elite converging upon the scene.

No long red carpet that led to His throne,
no ornate surroundings, no silk pillow to lay on.

God became flesh and dwelt among them,
so each man, woman, and child would come to Him.

It pleased the heavenly Father, in Him all fullness dwell,
the image of the invisible God, God with us, Emmanuel.

Giving praise, glory and honor as we receive heaven's best,
let us rejoice and join in with the angels and the rest . . .

THE SEARCH

True love is so hard for one to find,
someone like you to be so sweet and kind.

I've looked all over from place to place,
and there you were, your pretty little face.

I thought I could never find someone like you,
someone to be with me all the way through.

We have had some good and some bad times,
I thank you so much dear for being mine.

I've searched this world all over this you should know,
for I have so much love for you I need to show.

I looked day after day all over everywhere,
got to the last place and you were there.

The true love that I've found, I've searched every place,
and it was worth it for I found your pretty little face . . .

GREAT TREASURE

You opened heaven's great door for your faithful to come in,
thank you, Father, for your great gift to all men.

You sent to us a gift wrapped in humble swaddling attire,
let us along with heaven's host gather round him to admire.

Thank you for sending your dear Son, whom you delight,
to watch over each one of us every single night.

O sing unto the Lord a new song, O sing all ye earth,
for He is greatly to be praised for His amazing virgin birth.

Come let us adore him, the choirs will forever sing,
receive this eternal gift from the eternal King of Kings.

The depth of the riches of God's wisdom and His love,
He wants so much to shower you with His mercy from above.

He opens the door of heaven giving His greatest treasure,
O come all you faithful for in you He takes great pleasure . . .

HIS APPEALINGS

Seek first the Kingdom and His perfect will for you,
then the things you really need will be added too.

Don't you look upon the others with intent to judge,
my Father loves each one of us and doesn't hold a grudge.

Wide is the gate that leads to certain desolation,
narrow is His straightened gate leading to great salvation.

Big crowds began to follow marveling at His words and healings,
and it came to pass that Jesus ended all His appealings.

All of us are truly blessed having God Himself within,
as we yield ourselves to Christ who took away our sin.

By their fruit you shall know them if they be of me,
for evil can never come from one of my trees.

A righteous man builds his life upon my solid foundation,
a foolish man looks for self and suffers my condemnation . . .

PURE IN HEART

He taught them how to live this life so very clearly,
following Him were those who loved Him so dearly.

Blessed are the poor, the mourners and the meek,
they are the ones with broken hearts He set out to seek.

Blessed are the merciful and the pure in heart,
they shall obtain mercy and experience God at very start.

You are the salt of the earth His light to an evil generation,
let His light shine before them as you go into their nation.

Don't lay up earthly treasures that thieves break in and rob,
lay up treasures of love as you follow me to God.

But keep a line open to my Father each and every day,
in this manner I command is how you need to pray.

Loving our enemies even as we love our brothers,
forgive us our sins and teach us to forgive all others . . .

PRECIOUS HEART

I thank you my love for letting me be a part,
for opening up your sweet and precious heart.

I will love you always til the day I die,
believe me darling that is not a lie.

You were sent to me from God up above,
He knew I needed just you to love.

I don't know what I would do if I didn't have you,
but I know I could ask God to help me through.

I need you with me each and every day,
and I will love you every step of the way.

You will be the only one that I'll always love,
for you were sent to me from God up above.

It was meant to be just for you and me,
God put us together for our life to be . . .

TOUCHED US

Arise my dear children and be not afraid,
when fears and doubts overcome us, He rushes to our aid.

He loves and forgives us for those bad things we've done,
Yes, He embraces us like one of His frightened sons.

How precious are His thoughts of you and me,
His thoughts are greater than the sands of the sea.

When I awake, I know that I'm still with Him,
O God, how great is the large sum of them.

Let thy salvation O God set up on high,
for your righteousness is poured down from the sky.

Their hearts have raced, and their chest began to quake,
then their bones involuntarily began to shake.

Just as He comforts our fears even today,
Jesus came and touched us and had all this to say . . .

ANCIENT OF DAYS

His claims to be the Christ was laid bare for all to see,
as He was stripped and bleeding, suffering there on that tree.

If they would have known He was the Lord of all glory,
but they hardened their hearts to His majestic love story.

The ancient of days this awesome Son of Man,
could have called a legion of angels with a wave of His hand.

His passion, love, and truth He fully shared,
His word was a balm to those who despaired.

He gave peace to those who ranted and raved,
and delivered Himself up so we might be saved.

The very ones He wanted to release from sin's domain,
were consumed with jealousy and hate, almost insane.

He revealed to us God's precious and mysterious ways,
and there came to us those Ancient of Days . . .

THE CROWD

This was just another death in which they would partake,
they'd seen executions before nailed to the stake.

Through the tears He saw people standing in mud,
enjoying the sight of this man's blood.

They treated Him like a leper, mocked Him like a clown,
punched Him and whipped Him to the ground.

The crowd screamed to the Lord in a drunken stupor,
come down off that cross if you are so super.

This crowd gave proof that Satan was alive for sure,
these particular types of reprobates just isn't any cure.

Each and every time His broken heart strained a beat,
precious blood gushed from the spike holes in His feet.

There was the Lamb of God beaten black and blue,
with seconds to live, "He cried" "Forgive them they know not
what they do" . . .

OLD STONES

If these enormous, imposing stones could just talk,
they would cry out detailing each spot Jesus walked.

They would describe in great detail and emotion,
how the Master, not trying, would cause a commotion.

Yes, these old stones have many stories to tell,
these old stones would indeed cry out if you ever fail.

He was crucified according to God's master plan,
He was risen on the third day to save the lost man.

Everyone worldwide comes to weep and moan,
standing there one can hear all of nature's groans.

The stones would cry out loud how He trod the sorrowful way,
leaving bloody footprints on the stones of that very day.

Lamenting their persecution as one strong nation,
recalling the day, the Lord paid for our eternal salvation . . .

THE PRISONER

He stumbled into the house, man what happened to him,
his brothers slashed and beat him, but he forgave them.

Gazing upon His wounds up and down,
skin from his back grossly hanging to the ground.

Convicted of a crime impossible for Him to commit,
bloody patches on His face displaying bruises and dried spit.

He was now in prison to be punished further,
Jesus would suffer without even a murmur.

They offered up a choice of who would go free,
they said crucify Jesus, let His blood be on me.

It's high time that we call on Jesus to set us free,
for all of us have been bound don't you see.

Like the man on the cross while you still have a choice,
open up your heart and take heed of the Master's voice . . .

OLD CROSS

His beautiful yet sad eyes pierced my soul all the way,
I dreamed that I reached to touched Him that day.

I fell on my knees. He taken my sin,
and a thorn from His crown cut my skin.

The weight of the cross drove the needles in deeper,
as the Lord Jesus was becoming my Master and Keeper.

He drugged that old cross to the hill of the skull,
from that instance our life can never be dull.

In all His victory, He secured our salvation,
even our roughest times are caused for celebration.

So reach out and touch Him along your life's way,
let His precious blood cleanse your life if you may.

Let a thorn from His crown cut your skin,
fall on your knees and He'll take all your sin . . .

THIS VERY HOUR

His words were staggering and His message so grand,
as He passed rapidly before the very eyes of man.

Hearts were broken, replaced by new life for who believe,
He just went about doing cures to all who would receive.

Their spirits were dull and jealously filled them with hate,
covetousness only allowed them to persecute and debate.

Blessed be you after God for you shall all be filled,
and by His Holy Spirit you are all healed.

He said I'll be with you every day and night,
delivering us from darkness into His light.

They had finally gotten their own evil way,
so this pleading goes out to all men today.

You are worthy O Lord, to receive glory, honor, and power,
so listen to the Holy Spirit this very hour . . .

SALVATION

He secured my salvation at the cross,
for I was walking around this world lost.

The Lord of Glory died for you and me,
one minute mankind damned for an eternity.

But like flint, Christ set His face,
as the perfect lamb, His sacrificial grace.

He said my yoke is easy-come unto me,
for calvary's cross still set men free.

Yes, He arose on the third day exactly as He said,
It's me Jesus Christ I'm back from the dead.

Hope was lifted up they praised Him more,
the Lord was upon us all and yes even the poor.

Jesus returning in clouds, in power and glory,
then starts the last chapter of His eternal story . . .

ETERNAL FATE

He bore our griefs and carried our sorrows,
for our sin He was stricken, guaranteeing tomorrows.

Bowed His head and gave up the Ghost,
God's only Son whom He loved the most.

The hour has come the Son of Man should be glorified,
the Lord said concerning the resurrection after being crucified.

In Him was life and the life was the light of all men,
but those who loved evil could not comprehend.

Those who believed upon Him received grace upon grace,
while those who loved darkness would later spit in His face.

All of this was written so His followers may proclaim,
believing in Christ, the Son of God you might have life in His name.

There is no sin for which He has not paid,
have faith in God, In Christ you're saved . . .

SPECIAL DAY

Happy Birthday dear Toby, Happy Birthday to you,
this is your special day and I love you too.

Now you're a big boy who just turned seven,
the gift I give to you is from God in heaven.

April 27th is one to always remember,
I love that day more than the 25th of December.

I send this little note inside this birthday card,
enjoy this special day I know it's not hard.

This is just for you my little sugarbear,
just a little note to let you know I care.

I just want to give to you all the best wishes,
now that you're seven you can do the dishes.

So enjoy this day that belongs only to you,
and Toby my son remember, "I love you too" . . .

TURN TO ME

I know you see things looking very bad,
and I see that you and the family are sad.

Genni my child just takes your stand,
for all your problems are in my hands.

So don't you worry about what to do,
because Genni I am here to help you.

I'm telling you now don't you dare cry,
just ask of me and don't be shy.

I know what it is before you even ask,
I'm just asking you Genni to remove the mask.

I see all things that happen to you,
believe me child I will help you through.

So will you now Genni just turn to me,
let me get started so things can be . . .

LITTLE FRIENDS

Kimber and Shelby, you are so so sweet,
having you as my little friends I think is neat.

You will always be with me in my heart and prayers.
I just want you to know that God is there.

I want you to know that Jesus loves you,
no matter what it is He will help you through.

Will you, Kimber, remember me when you pray,
just ask God our Father what you should say.

And to you little Shelby always stay true,
don't ever forget that God loves you.

Kimber and Shelby, you mean a lot to me,
I have you in my heart and there you will be.

I just want you both to know that you are so sweet,
and with you as my little friends it's very neat.

MOM'S SPECIAL DAY

I'm writing this little note just for you today,
so sit down and relax mom I have something to say.

Happy Mother's Day to you "oh" Happy Mother's Day to you,
I thank you mom for always guiding me through.

You are the best mom for any child,
yes, even the ones that always run wild.

Your love and kindness oh it's so so sweet,
you never gave up and I think that's neat.

I know that you will be there to always care,
for you're the best mom with love to share.

I close now for that's what I had to say,
so Happy Mother's Day to you on this special day.

Hold on there mom before you go rest,
I want to tell you that you're the best . . .

FORGET NOT YET

Forget not yet the tried intent,
my great travail so gladly spent.

The weary life you know, since when,
the suit, the service, none tell can.

The painful patience in all delays,
the cruel wrongs, the scornful ways.

Forget not yet, forget not this,
the mind that never means amiss.

The vain travail has wearied me so sore,
but as for me I may no more.

I am of them that furthest come behind,
yet may I by no means my wearied mind.

Forget not then thy own approved,
whose steadfast faith yet never moved . . .

BY CHANCE

They flee from me that sometime did I seek,
I have seen them gentle, tame, and meek.

That now are wild and do not remember,
with sinful foot stalking in my chamber.

They take bread at my hand and now they range,
busily seeking with a continual change.

Into a strange fashion of forsaking,
it was no dream; I lay broad waking.

Proud of the spoil that thou hast got,
think now he hath his bow forgot.

But since he is so kindly served,
I would know now what he has deserved.

The time that thou have lost and always spent,
and then by chance bring them to repent . . .

SAW THE WORLD

My feast of joy is but a dish of pain,
all my good is but vain hope of gain.

My tale was heard and yet it was not told,
my youth is spent and yet I am not old.

My fruit has fallen and yet my leaves are green,
I saw the world and yet I was not seen.

I looked for life and saw it was a shade,
and now I die, and I was now but made.

My prime of youth is but a frost of cares,
my crop of corn is but a field of tares.

I sought my death; and found it in my womb,
I trod the earth and knew it was my tomb.

My thread is cut and yet it is not spun,
and now I live and now my life is done . . .

THESE DAYS

How many of the foolish, painted things
shall be forgotten, whom no poet sings.

When nothing else remains from these days,
upon the alms of my superfluous praise.

To have seen thee this world's only glory,
shall be so much delighted with this story.

They shall grieve they lived not in these times,
all adults and kids reading these rhymes.

I am glad, yes glad, with all my heart,
that there's help and these rhymes are a part.

When his pulse failing, passion speechless lies,
and the innocence is closing up his eyes.

But it was not seen in either of our brows,
so shake hands forever, cancel all our vows . . .

SILENT THOUGHT

Shall I compare you to a summer day,
rough winds do shake the darling buds of May.

Sometimes to hot the eye of heaven shines,
and every fair from fair sometimes declines.

I all alone weep my outcast state,
and look upon myself and curse my fate.

Yet in these thoughts myself almost despising,
like to the lark at break of day arising.

When to the sessions of sweet silent thoughts,
I sigh the lack of many a thing I sought.

Full many a glorious morning have I seen,
kissing with golden face the meadows green.

This thought is as a death which cannot choose,
but weep to have that which it fears to lose . . .

PLEASING SOUND

Not my own fears nor the prophetic soul,
can yet the lease of my true love control.

Now with the drops of this most balmy time,
since, spite of him, I'll live in this poor rhyme.

Love's not time's fool, though rosy lips and cheeks,
love alters not with his brief hours and weeks.

Past reason hunted and no sooner had,
on purpose laid to make the taker mad.

I have seen roses demasked, red and white,
and in some perfumes is there more delight.

That music has a far more pleasing sound,
as when she walks treads on the ground.

Yet, by heaven, I think my love is rare,
as a lady, belied with false compare . . .

HONOR AND GRACE

Take you a course, get you a place,
observe His honor, and His grace.

Soldiers find wars and lawyers find out still,
when did the heat which my veins fill.

Call us what you will, we are made such by love,
and we in us find the eagle and the dove.

Countries, towns, courts beg from above,
for a pattern of you and your love.

Fruits of much grief they are emblems of more,
when a tear falls, that thou fall which it bore.

A globe, yes world, by that impression grow,
till your tears mixed with mine do overflow.

Let me pour forth my tears before thy face,
to observe your honor and your grace . . .

STOLEN JOY

To all our world of well stolen joy,
tell him we now can show him more.

He slept and dreamed of no such thing,
and kissed the cradle of our King.

Which to be seen needs not His light,
then He ever showed to mortal sight.

The babe looked up and showed his face,
gloomy night embraced the wonderful place.

By those sweet eyes was persuasive powers,
where He meant frost, He scattered flowers.

To furnish the fair infant's little bed,
come hovering over the place's head.

Great little one, whose embracing birth,
lifts earth to heaven, stoops heaven to earth . . .

WORLD'S SIN

What shall I say my Lord, with what begin,
the world is saddle backed with the loads of sin.

To overflow and drown the world, yes, all drowned,
and overflown with sin that doth abound.

Thy human nature "oh" choice timber rich,
with dressing of the Holy Spirit's pitch.

Take me, my Lord, into thy golden ark,
though hell spews streams of flames and the heaven sparks.

I'll make thy curled flames my citterns wire,
to toss my songs of praise rung on them higher.

The world without the sun is as dungeon dark,
the moon and stars are but as chilly sparks.

All light delights yet dozed wood-light is cold,
as lamp and glow-worm light the stars do hold . . .

THE STORM

There was a roaring in the winds all night,
but now the sun is rising calm and bright.

All things that love the sun are out of doors,
the grass is bright with rain drops on the moors.

The pleasant season did my heart employ,
heard them not, as happy as a boy.

I heard the skylark warbling in the sky,
even such a happy child of earth am I.

My whole life I have lived in pleasant thought,
as if needful things would come unsought.

Now, whether it were by peculiar grace,
yet it befell that in this lonely place.

But there came in the end despondency and madness,
and we poets in our youth begin with gladness . . .

THE QUESTION

Upon a long grey staff of shaven wood,
motionless as a cloud the young man stood.

Stirred with his staff, and fixedly did look,
as if he had been reading in a book.

Drawing to his side, to him did say,
this morning gives us promise of a glorious day.

In courteous speech which forth he slowly drew
this is a lonesome place for one like you.

The young man still stood talking by my side,
scarce heard; nor word for word could I divide.

My former thoughts returned; the fear that kills,
cold pain, and labor, and all fleshly ills.

My question eagerly did I then renew,
how is it that you live, and what is it that you do???

LOVE SO SUDDEN

I never was struck before that hour,
her face it bloomed like a sweet flower.

With love so sudden and so sweet,
it stole my heart away complete.

My legs refused to turn and walk away,
my life and all seemed turned to clay.

Words from my eyes did I start,
and the blood burnt round my heart.

She seemed to hear my silent voice,
is she the flower for this man's choice.

I never saw so sweet of a face,
my heart has left its dwelling place.

My face turned pale as deadly pale,
and when she looked what could I ail . . .

GOD'S GATE

To all my friends in the Lord Jesus Christ,
you don't have to worry He paid the price.

We look toward heaven to see God's Gate,
hoping and praying that it's not too late.

My dear friends always stay strong,
and I promise you God won't steer you wrong.

Just hold your head up, keep Him in mind,
for we all know God's not hard to find.

You are in each and every prayer,
don't ever think that God's not fair.

He will pick you up whenever you fall,
what are you waiting for, make the call.

You are my friends through Jesus Christ,
don't ever forget He was sent to pay the price . . .

DELIGHTS TO FILL

I looked to find a man who walked with God,
though gladdened millions on His footstool trod.

Like the translated patriarch of old,
yet none with Him did such sweet converse hold.

I heard the wind in low complaint go by,
day unto day spoke wisdom from on high.

That none it's melodies like Him could hear,
yet none like David turned a willing ear.

For Him no heart-built temple open stood,
had hewn Him lofty shrines of stone and wood.

The only temple He delights to fill,
is left unfinished and in ruins still.

God walked alone unhonored through the earth,
the soul forgetful of her noble birth . . .

GOD'S CHORES

I sit here alone with my Lord Jesus Christ,
thinking about how He paid such wonderful price.

He paid it for you and me this you should know,
just to show us which way we should go.

I will love the Lord with all my heart,
for He has promised to do His part.

I give my heart to you today,
to cleanse it Lord and have your way.

Take away the old, replace it with new,
for I live for you Lord and only you.

I belong to you now, I am yours,
teach my Lord to do your chores.

I thank you lord for sending your Son,
and I love you for what you've done . . .

GOD'S PARTY

I went to a party in a county jail,
if we don't change our ways we're going to hell.

This is not the way life should be,
open your eyes so that you can see.

Jesus came down for one reason only,
that's so you won't be so lonely.

I'm not afraid to bow down on my knees,
to ask the Lord to save me please.

Guide me through the thick and the thin,
and forgive me God for my sin.

Save me now from the burning fire,
stay away Satan for you are a liar.

I belong to God once and for all,
and I know He still cares when I fall...

CHRIST TELLS US

Take heed this day and discern the Master's voice,
for Christ gave to all a real choice.

You have this very day, so seize it right now,
confess Christ as Lord, fall down and humbly bow.

There are no guarantees you'll be here tomorrow,
avoid at all cost that horrendous day of sorrow.

Be renewed in the Spirit Christ tells us,
angels will sever the wicked from among the just.

An angel grabbed hold of Satan casting him in a pit alone,
the beast was taken and thrown alive into hot brimstone.

Partying all the way to their own hearse,
ignoring the perilous horror of God's universe.

God awaits the lost whose time has expired,
whosoever was not found in the book fell into the lake of fire . . .

CONVERSATION

I close my eyes to say a little prayer,
to let my Father know that I do care.

While I was talking to my Lord God,
my heart took off and began to trod.

Before I knew it, I was in deep conversation,
asking the Father what happened to this nation.

The Father said, all things you see are but a show,
to let the world know how things will go.

It's all going according to His plan,
for you see it's all in God's hand.

So don't you dare get in His way,
Jesus Christ is here and here to stay.

Look at us now what do we see,
the world changing to the way it should be . . .

THE WHISPER

How can I Lord God please you today,
I'm asking you to show me the way.

You know it's hard in this sinful place,
look at me Lord, look at my face.

I'm trying you know to please only you,
send me an angel to guide me through.

I'm walking a straight line and then I fall,
yes, Lord Father I hear you whenever you call.

Time after time it's the same old sin,
help me Father for I am your kin.

I read your words all through the day,
now teach me to know what they say.

So how can I lord God please you this day,
whisper in my ear what you need me to say . . .

STOOD BY ME

For all those times you stood by me,
for all the truth you made me see.

You were my strength when I was weak,
even my voice when I couldn't speak.

You gave me wings and made me fly,
touched my hand, I could touch the sky.

You stood by me, and I stood tall,
I had your love, I had it all.

You were my eyes when I couldn't see,
and you saw the best there was in me.

Through the lies you were always true,
my world is a better place because of you.

You're the one who saw me through it all,
you held me up and never let me fall . . .

HOMEWARD BOUND

Thank you, Jesus, Thank you Lord,
send me your Spirit along with sword.

I need you now to save my soul,
give to me Father a brand-new goal.

Teach me to pray to you each day,
help me Lord learn what to say.

I need your guidance in this place,
for one day soon I will win this race.

Homeward bound then I will go,
for my Lord father told me so.

His Kingdom is waiting up above,
oh, my Father has so much love.

So here I come to you one day,
thank you, Jesus, for paying my way . . .

HARD TIME

Here I am just once again.
writing you this with paper and pen.

I don't know where I went wrong,
but here I am singing this prison song.

I'm down here again doing hard time,
keep telling myself things will be fine.

This time it's harder I want you to know,
for I'm stuck in this place nowhere to go.

I don't know what keeps bringing me back,
maybe it's confidence that I lack.

I'm trying real hard to do this time,
but I don't think it should be mine.

Here I am just once again,
writing to you from the pen . . .

SOMETHING TO SAY

Why is it we wait until we're sad,
to see that things are going bad.

All our life we didn't want any help.
but standing with us, the promise God kept.

Even though we weren't living the way we should,
the angel with us kept telling us that we could.

We were so hardheaded we didn't hear when he said,
you are all new now, for the old is dead.

We have times that we want our way,
but there comes Jesus with something to say.

Don't you dare go back to being the old you,
for I was sent to guide you through.

Whenever you need me just call out my name,
for you and I child, we are the same . . .

WHY-O-WHY

Here it is another year gone by,
we're asked this one question and it's "why",

We have been told that Christ died for us,
but here we are still putting up a fuss.

Why-O-why does it seem so hard,
we all know that God is the number one card.

Can we promise to have a better year,
for you know Jesus Christ is very dear.

Would you look at the things we would have done,
if God our Father didn't send Jesus Christ His son.

So let's make this year living the way we should,
for Jesus Christ died on the cross so we could.

Forgive us Lord God from all our sin,
and let us be your very own kin . . .

ON THIS DAY

This is a day we all will celebrate,
for it is said to be Christ's birth date.

December 25th we all should know,
we get together to see a Christmas show.

I just want to say Merry Christmas to you,
for Christ was born to guide us through.

I wish I was there to see the sight,
even go around to see the Christmas lights.

This is a Christmas for us to remember,
it's on this day the 25th of December.

So Merry Christmas to you once again I say,
whatever you do don't forget this day.

This is a day that God has made,
there is a manger Jesus Christ was laid . . .

OUR FRIENDSHIP

A friend is someone who is always there,
to show each other that they really do care.

You my friend have done just that,
so to you my friend I tip my hat.

Weezie my friend you mean the world to me,
in this poem I hope you will see.

Friends like you are hard to come by,
when I think of you, I seem to cry.

There is one more thing before I go,
Weezie my friend I want you to know.

God put you in my life for a reason
He looks after me while I'm in prison.

So I will do for you just as I'm told,
for our friendship together I will hold.

Your friendship means the world to me,
I just hope it will last and always be . . .

THIS MAN CHRIST

Things may seem hard at times for you,
you may even think you can't make it through.

But let me tell you about this man that I know,
he is someone who will guide you everywhere you go.

You might even know him, His name is Jesus Christ,
He died on the cross, He paid a great price.

So whenever you feel like you're down and out,
just look up to heaven and give God a shout.

He knows all things, yes even the bad,
but He will always comfort you whenever you're sad.

So when you think that things are hard for you,
close your eyes and remember what Jesus went through.

You have nothing to worry about with this man Christ,
for He loves you so or He wouldn't have paid that price . . .

GLORIOUS SIGHT

Behold, we bring you a good tiding,
said the angel as he came out of hiding.

You'll find the child wrapped in swaddling clothes,
take Him your offering if only a desert rose.

In ecstatic excitement off toward the stable they went,
an umblemished lamb from the flock to present.

Little lambs on their shoulders they came to the resting place,
standing as close as they could to see His immaculate face.

In that child was life and the life was the light of all men,
that light shined through darkness though some could not comprehend.

Yes, the world still celebrates that Bethlehem glory,
proclaiming with those shepherds that sweet Christmas story.

Recounting how He sent His word to heal all of mankind,
setting us free, giving spiritual sight to all were blind . . .

JUST LOOK

If you could just look into my heart,
you will see Lord God I will do my part.

I'm sitting in this building I feel all alone,
asking myself, Lord, where have you gone.

It seems to me that you're far far away,
come to me Jesus and please come to stay.

What can I do Lord to show that I love you,
for I need your help to get me through.

I know that I can do all things in your name,
for Jesus has said this is no game.

As each day goes by my faith will grow,
for I see the light of Jesus He lets it glow.

I'm asking you again just look into my heart,
come to me Jesus and give me a new start . . .

COMPLETED PLAN

In agony from the cross He looked down,
soldiers at His feet gathered round.

Through hot tears He saw others standing in the mud,
insults and curses enjoying the sight of His blood.

Just another day on the hill for the ghouls,
oh, how could these people be such fools.

They brutalized their Messiah and put Him to death,
slashed Him with whips, He could barely catch His breath.

The glorious light that once shined from His face,
was given to cover mans sin and pitiful disgrace.

God of all creation had turned His face from His dear Son,
opening the door to heaven bidding all to simply come.

He had successfully completed His unbelievably hard plan,
of rescuing this hell-bound race of rebellious, sinful man . . .

TREASURES

He taught them how to live this life so very clearly,
there following Him were those who loved Him dearly.

Blessed are the poor, the mourners and the meek,
they're the ones with broken hearts, I set out to seek.

Blessed are the merciful and the pure in heart,
they shall experience God at the very start.

You're the salt of the earth, My light to an evil generation
let your light shine before them as you go into their nation.

Don't lay up earthly treasures that thieves will rob,
lay up treasures of love as you follow me all the way to God.

Keep a line open to my Father each and every day,
in this manner I command is how you should pray.

Loving our enemies even as we love our brothers,
forgive us our sins and teach us to forgive all others . . .

THE WATERS

The current of the Jordan, how swiftly do you run,
flowing water of the river that washed God's precious Son.

How beautiful you break forth from the sparkling sea of Galilee,
racing out into the lonely desert for all to see.

The story of the Savior baptized out from your flowing banks,
of John, the baptizer, looking into heaven giving thanks.

Lovingly and obediently, He plunged into your water,
submitting to the wishes of His beloved. Heavenly Father.

The Father loves the Son and has given all things into His hand,
giving Him authority and judgement because He is the Son of Man.

God sent not His Son to the world to condemn all who rant and rave,
only they believe upon Him, and that the world might be saved.

Who is he that comes of the wilderness like pillars of smoke so brave,
traveling in greatness of his strength, so powerful to save . . .

RIGHT AND WRONG

Never was seen such an angel-eyes of heavenly blue,
features that shamed Apollo, hair of a golden hue.

The woman simply adored him, his lips were like cupids bow,
but he never ventured to use them, so they voted him slow.

Till at last there came one woman a marvel of loveliness,
and whispered to him, do you love me, He answered Yes.

Put your arm around me, kiss me, and hold me so,
but fiercely he drew back saying this thing is wrong and I know.

We have outlived the old standards, like an overtight thong,
the ancient outworn, puritanic traditions of right and wrong.

The Master feared for His angel and called him to His side,
for oh, the woman was wondrous, and oh, the angel was tried.

Deep in his hell sang the devil, this was the strain of his son,
the ancient outworn, puritanic traditions of right and wrong . . .

JESUS CHRIST THE SAVIOUR IS BORN

Do you recall the joy and excitement when the child came at his birth,
you see, God sent His only Son to be born on this earth.

For unto you in the city of David a savior shall be born and thus,
his name shall be called Emmanuel, which means "God with us".

An angel appeared unto Mary and told her of God's plan,
she would be the mother of Jesus, a virgin who had never known a man.

Now when Mary's time had fully come and the child of God was born
of them,
it was in a lowly manger in the city of Bethlehem.

Wise men came to the manger with treasures of gold, frankincense
and myrrh,
precious gifts for the baby Jesus, worshipping Him on the day of His
birth.

Christmas is about Jesus and how we celebrate the day of his birth,
how the angel's told of Him coming when our Savior came to earth.

When you celebrate this Christmas, I'd like to say what it is worth,
Jesus left the glory of heaven in order for us to experience the NEW
BIRTH . . .

IF I WERE AN ANGEL

If I were an angel this is what I would do,
I would spread God's love and be your angel too.

You were put in my life as a precious gift,
for God has seen that your spirit needed a lift.

Don't get me wrong for you have helped me too,
so don't you worry my friend God will be blessing you.

If you ever need me or just want to talk,
just think of you and your angel taking a walk.

I will always be with you in your heart,
for God, He put me there to be a part.

If I were an angel, I would be holding your hand,
walking with you as you're walking through the sand.

So if ever you need me just call out my name,
for when I became an angel mine and God's became the same . . .

YOU'RE SO SPECIAL

You're so special I just want you to know,
so open your heart and let His precious love flow.

It's the hard times in life when we need His help,
but we always need the promise that He has kept.

He has promised to us His amazing grace,
for you my friend are special in His heavenly place.

Not only will He love you through all of this mess,
He will help you through it and make the problems less.

So I hope you see just how special you are,
for whenever you need help remember He's not far.

Understand this now and don't change your mind,
for you my friend God made one of a kind.

He has made you in such a very special way,
and that is how you should always want to stay . . .

THROUGH THE HARD TIMES

God sent His only Son to make a path for us,
He worked so hard, and we did nothing but fuss.

He had trials and tribulations throughout His stay,
went through the hard times to show us the way.

He did all of this, so you and I didn't have to,
and to show just how much he really loves you.

He knows that we all go through the hard times,
He is walking with us so we don't lose our minds.

So the next time that you feel all down and out,
just look up to heaven and give Jesus a shout.

He will tap you on your shoulder to let you know He's there,
and give you a hug to show that He does care.

We all go through the hard times on our way,
but don't you worry, Jesus came to stay . . .

COMPLETELY

Lift up your hands to the holy sky,
things are happening to you, and you know why.

There are things in your life I do not approve of,
get rid of them now my child to receive my love.

I will not give to you more than you can bare,
I am letting you know child that I do care.

So will you please give them up and live for me,
I don't mean some, I mean all of them completely.

I will restore your life and give unto you,
all the things that you need even some new.

Listen my child I'm knocking on your door,
I know you love me, for you showed me before.

So turn from this world and give it up today,
grab my hand, walk with me I will lead the way . . .

THE CALL FROM GOD

Hello, this is God, I'm calling to see if you're there,
for I'm sending you a message to let you know I care.

I have been calling but you won't answer your phone,
I want you to know child that I'm not gone.

If ever you need me just give me a call,
and I will pick you up whenever you fall.

You can always reach me through this line,
any place, any reason, and at any time.

I just wish that you would answer your phone,
to let me know that you want to come home.

I have tried calling you time and time again,
all I want is for you to confess your sin.

I don't care what time of day that you call me,
just as long as you do so I can help you see . . .

PRECIOUS LOVE

I come to you child from the Father above,
to let you know about His great precious love.

He loves you so much He sent His only Son,
to die on a cross for what we have done.

He then raised Him from the grave on the third day,
to show you child there is a better way.

He walked about the earth healing the sick and blind,
spreading the Father's Gospel and keeping you in mind.

He promised to you a place with the Father,
and while doing all His miracles it was no bother.

He was the only one on earth who never did sin,
even when He was beaten near death and thrown in the pen.

So I came to you child from our Father above,
to walk about the earth and spread His precious love . . .

BLINDED

I will walk with thee all the days of my life,
and treat you Lord Jesus as my sweet precious wife.

You have come to this earth to be with me,
for I was blinded by the world and could not see.

You opened my eyes, and you walked me through,
and that is one reason Jesus, that I love you.

You stood with me all through the way,
always having something positive to say.

You never did leave me when I stumbled and fell,
you always picked me up, you saved me from hell.

You tended to me because I am your child,
touched my heart when I was running wild.

There will never be a day where I will deny you,
for you died on that cross because of what I do . . .

A BIRTHDAY GIFT

You're a very special person who deserves the best,
this is your day Weezie so take you a rest.

It's your birthday and I wanted to say,
you are very special to me, and I like it that way.

So I send this little note in this birthday card,
saying, enjoy your day Weezie I know it's not hard.

God is throwing you a party in heaven above,
giving you the best gift of all, "His precious love".

Weezie my friend I wish I could be there,
but I want you to know that I really do care.

The only gift that I can give is from God above,
and that's all my prayers, thoughts, and love.

So Happy Birthday to you again I will say,
hope you enjoy it Weezie, have a great day . . .

NEEDED A FRIEND

You are someone so special whom I love so dear,
in my heart you will be forever so near.

God put you in my life because I needed a friend,
now we can go to places that we've never been.

You have been there when times were so hard,
and all I can do is send you a little card.

I want you to know Weezie you mean the world to me,
for you are my sweet friend I hope you can see.

Together we will be no matter how far apart,
for you my friend will always be in my heart.

Friends like you are so hard to find,
someone so sweet and a heart so kind.

You opened your heart and placed me in there,
just for that I know you really do care.

Weezie my friend you are special to me,
and that you see is how it's always going to be . . .

LOOK WHAT JESUS CAN DO

When I was lost and lonely and could not find a friend,
I prayed to God every day to bring these feelings to an end.

Then I met you and I saw something in your eyes,
it was the peace I needed, oh thank you Jesus for this surprise.

I was given someone who is very very dear,
Jesus has filled their heart with so much cheer.

When you need help look what Jesus can do,
He will pour out His blessing and provide for you.

I'm so happy that our great friendship began,
I just thank Jesus for you over and over again.

He has sent me an angel from heaven and it's you,
oh, want you just look what Jesus can do . . .

Written by: Roger Johnston and Louise Miller

VALENTINE'S DAY WITH JESUS

Jesus does not send perfume to linger in the air,
He sends salvation, sweet to show how much He cares.

He doesn't bring me candy hearts in boxes of delight,
instead, He always lets me know I'm precious in His sight.

He doesn't send out pretty cards trimmed in shades of red,
instead, He gave His life for me, His precious blood was shed.

He doesn't hand out fancy gifts like we send to mother,
instead, He sends a message clear to always love each other.

He doesn't give teddy bears that whimper, "please be mine",
instead, He gave His heart to me, I wear it all the time.

He doesn't give out roses, pink for all the world to see,
instead, He gave eternal life, that's good enough for me . . .

WHAT IS A FRIEND?

A friend is someone who is there when you call,
someone to lift you up whenever you fall.

Weezie my friend that is what I will do for you,
I will help you up and try to get you through.

I am here for you if ever you need me,
that my friend is how it will always be.

Even if the times seem to be rough,
together as friends should be enough.

Together as friends we can get through it all,
so Weezie my friend I am here if ever you call.

A friend is someone that you can depend on,
Weezie my friend I will never leave you alone.

So call on me if ever you need to,
for I am your friend, and I will help you through . . .

A MOTHER'S LOVE

A mother's love is something that no-one can explain,
it's made of deep devotion and sacrifice and pain.

It is endless and unselfish and enduring come what may,
for nothing can destroy it or take that love away.

It is patient and forgiving when all others are forsaking,
it never fails or falters even though the heart is breaking.

It believes beyond believing when the world around condemns,
it glows with all the beauty of the rarest, brightest gems.

It is far beyond defining, it defies all explanation,
and it still remains a secret like the mysteries of creation.

A many splendored miracle man cannot understand,
another wondrous evidence of God's tender guiding hand . . .

SWEET VALENTINE

Here it is the fourteenth of February to thousand and nine,
and I'm asking you Weezie would you be my Valentine.

You are so special to me, and you will always be a part,
for this year will be a brand-new start.

I give to you a big hug and maybe a kiss too,
Weezie my friend this Valentine's just for you.

I was your Valentine in the year two thousand eight,
and one day soon we will be going on that date.

So I ask you now Weezie to be my sweetheart,
if you say yes, well, that would be a great start.

I send with this note a great big hug and kiss,
to let you know that it is you that I miss.

So Weezie my sweetheart will you be my Valentine,
on this special day in February two thousand and nine.

DREAM COME TRUE

Throughout life we find someone special to love,
someone who is an angel sent from God up above.

We can't show each other how much love is inside,
and it's not the love that anyone can hide.

I just wish that I could show how I love you,
one day soon God will make that dream come true.

We both know that love never works being far apart,
but I can promise you now, you're always in my heart.

If it's meant to be then God will put us there,
to show each other just how much we do care.

You were put in my life for some unknown reason,
and I'm sure that it wasn't just for one season.

I know you love me so stop putting up such a fuss,
for God gave you me and me to you, He did it for us . . .

THE CROSS

There is a man who died on a cross,
He died for me and all that are lost.

His name is Jesus Christ, this I now know,
He said He came to give life to all that would go.

We should always remember the cross on the hill,
for Jesus hung there for us to pay our bill.

No other man would do as Jesus did,
the clothes He died in were put up for bid.

There is no other love as strong as this man's,
want you now reach out and take His hands.

You can't go wrong when you accept His grace,
for when you do, he will take you to a wonderful place.

So when you start to go wrong just think of that cross,
and the one who died there when you were lost . . .

SENT FROM GOD

I needed someone to help me get through,
and out of nowhere God sent me you.

He knew I needed someone who would be there,
someone with love, someone who would care.

I knew I didn't deserve an angel such as this,
but there is something He has He didn't want me to miss.

I don't know just yet what that might be,
but I am glad that God sent you to me.

This is a walk that I cannot ever forget,
and you my friend are an important part of it.

He knew I needed someone to lift me up when I'm down,
someone to pull me out of the water when I begin to drown.

So you are my angel sent from God up above,
and I will love and cherish you for you were sent with love . .

MY DREAM– I CAN

The Lord came to me the other night in a dream,
I saw my Savior Jesus Christ hanging from a beam.

He told me to go out and spread His Good News,
and said that I could do it by starting with you.

He was sent to this earth to live as a man,
to save and forgive and to let us know that we can.

Fight His battle, not worry about winning,
for He has conquered it from the beginning.

He also said to stand up tall and high,
for His coming again is at nigh.

So I am here to tell you about a man I know,
His name is Jesus Christ and He is the way to go.

Then I woke up with the Lord's sword in hand,
knowing and believing, no matter what, I CAN . . .

FRIEND FOR LIFE

When life seems to be at its end,
remember one thing, you have a friend.

I will be with you every step of the way,
I am your friend from God, I'm here to stay.

If ever you need a shoulder to lean on to,
always known that I'm here just for you.

I know it's hard to find a friend that's true,
but God sent me to you to help you through.

You will always have a special place in my heart,
for God put you there to be a part.

So always know I'm a friend for life,
can't cut this friendship with a sharp knife.

If ever you need to talk just pick up your pen,
I am here forever; I am your friend . . .

SOMEONE CARES

Someone care's and always will,
the world forgets but God loves them still.

You cannot go beyond this someone's love,
no matter what you're guilty of.

For God forgives until the very end,
He is your one faithful, loyal friend.

Though you try to hide your face,
there is no shelter in any place.

No one can escape His watchful eye,
not on this earth, nor in the sky.

He's ever present and always there,
to take you and me in His tender care.

Someone cares and loves you still,
and God's the someone who always will . . .

IF YOU HAD A FRIEND

If you had a friend, strong, simple, true,
who believed in the very best of you.

Who knew your thoughts and who understood,
and who cared for you as a father would.

Who would stick by you to the very end,
I am sure you would try to please your friend.

Supposed your friend was high and great,
and sat like a king in shining state.

He lived in a palace rich and tall,
and His praise was loud on the lips of all.

When he turned to you and you alone,
and He called you up to His golden throne.

He singled you out from all the crowd,
oh, wouldn't you just be jolly proud . . .

9 781637 513538